Adult coloring book

BY

TANYA BOGEMA (STOLOVA)

Our group in facebook:
https://www.facebook.com/groups/1280996941971412/

Hi! My name is Tatiana and I'm painter :)
Thank you so much that you are choosing my books in spite of many other books present on market. I really appreciate this. Every time I start new project I think about how to make my book more interesting. And I can't do this without you. To do that I need to have your feedbacks. Communication with you is very very important for creation process. With your feedbacks you give me new ideas and inspiration for new books that become better and more interesting.
Sincerely yours, Tatiana.

Nice Little Town 4 - Adult Coloring Book
Copyright © 2018 by Tatiana Bogema (Stolova)

ISBN: 978-1984923257

THIS BOOK BELONGS TO

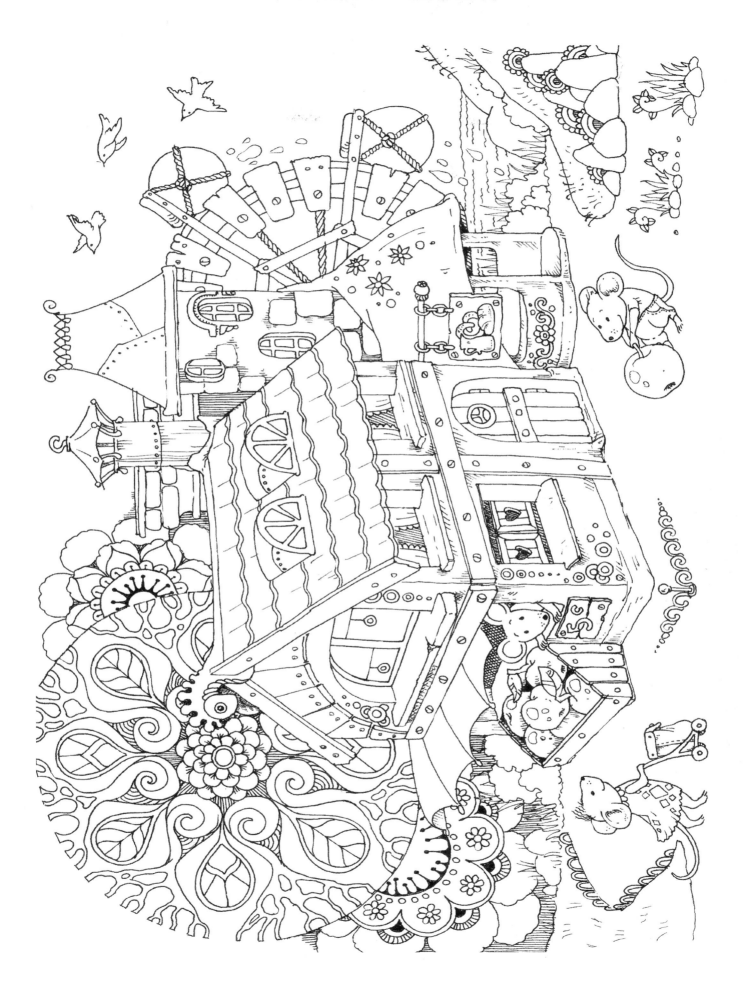

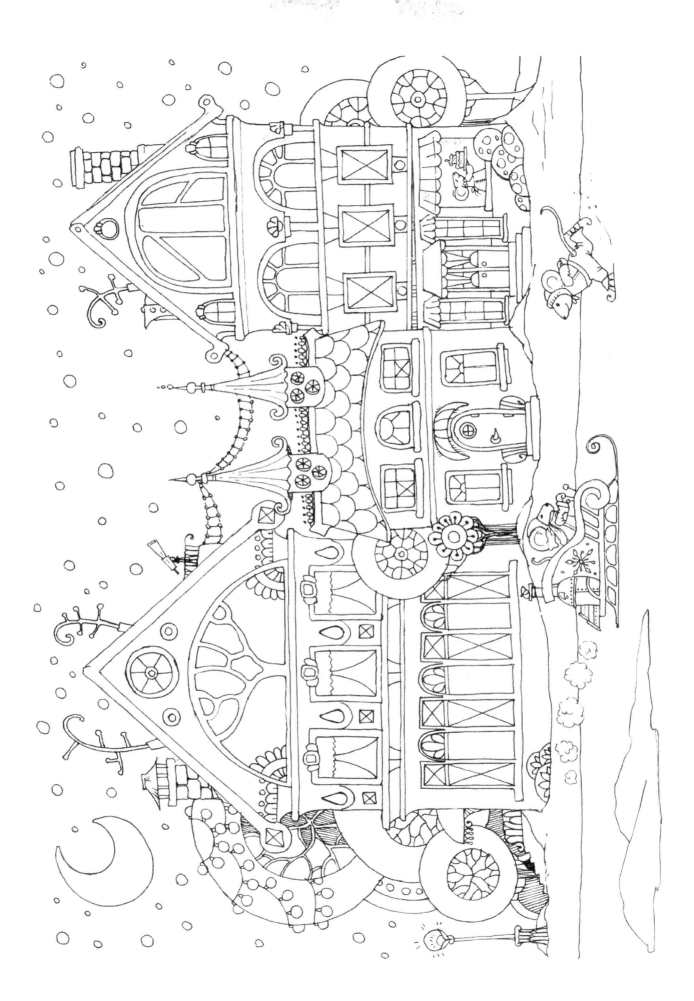

ILLUSTRATIONS
FROM
OTHER
MY
BOOKS

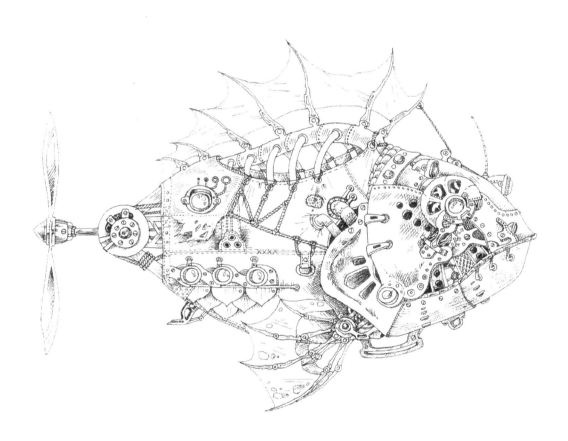

CUTE GIRLS

NICE
LITTLE
TOWN
2

NICE LITTLE TOWN 3

Adult coloring book by Tanya Bogema (Stolova)

NICE
LITTLE TOWN
CHRISTMAS

Adult coloring book   by Tanya Bogema (Stolova)

NICE
LITTLE TOWN
EASTER

MAGIC
MASK

GREAT
LIONS

STEAMPUNK

STEAMPUNK
VOL 2

AWESOME
ANIMALS

NICE LITTLE
DRAGONS

FOR VALENTINE, WITH LOVE!

Made in the USA
Lexington, KY
16 April 2018